Wyoming State Capitol

Cheyenne

Jane Moorman

There is a saying, "It was a Friday night and it seemed like a good idea at the time." That sums up the beginning of the State Capitols Project.

When I told my brother of my idea of photographing state capitols, he said, "You do know there are 50 states and two of them you can't drive to."

Each capitol has its own unique beauty that reflects the state's personality when it was built.

Jane Moorman, photographer

Wyoming Statehouse

Wyoming, known as the "Equality State," claims the distinction of being the first state to allow women the right to vote, beginning when it was a territory.

Fifty years before the passage of the 19th Amendment to the U.S. Constitution, women in the territory were voting.

Established as a territory in 1869, Wyoming quickly garnered national attention when the first territorial assembly granted all women above the age of 21 the right to vote.

The suffrage act was motivated by a number of factors, including enticing more women to the territory to increase the population, bringing in more voters, and genuine concerns that women should be allowed to vote.

Esther Morris was the territory's first female to hold the public office of justice of the peace in early 1870 at the age of 55.

Morris is notable because of her excellent performance in this office and her advocacy for women's suffrage both in the territory and, later, around the nation.

That distinction is honored with a statue of her commemorating her efforts to enact women's suffrage legislation which was approved by the Wyoming Territorial legislature in 1899.

The most recent statuary addition to the capitol building is The Four Sisters overlooking the rotunda from niches on the third floor, which remained empty for 133 years until 2019. See the statues on Page 9 and 10.

American sculptor Delissalde's bronze statues, with 24-carat gold embellishments, represent key values and attributes of Wyoming and its citizens.

The oldest sister, "Truth," leads the way, illuminating the path for Wyoming's pioneers. Next, "Justice"" sets the course for Wyomingites to live freely and peacefully. "Courage" encouraging and supporting citizens through hard times.

They youngest sister, "Hope," inspires the citizens to continue striving for the future, building the Wyoming founding leaders aspired for.

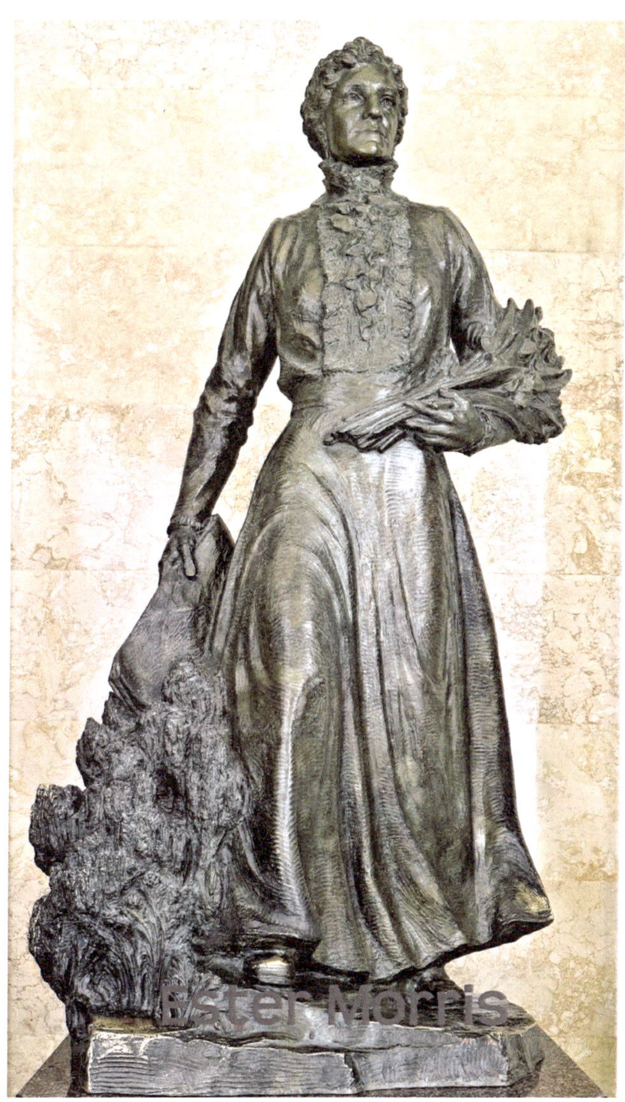

During restoration of the capitol, Ever-Greene Architectural Arts discovered original paintings on six vaults. Over the decades the doors have been painted several times with the most recent coat being dull brown covering the elaborate gold leaf decorations framing the six paintings.

Decorative Carvings

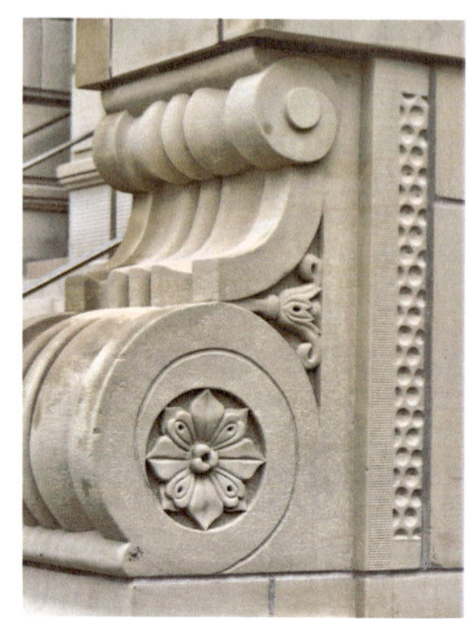

Unlike other state capitols, Wyoming used native sandstone from Rawlings, Wyoming, and Ft. Collins, Colorado, for the construction of its building capitol.

The Renaissance Revival style building was designed by architect David W. Gibbs & Company.

The cornerstone was laid on May 8, 1887, while Wyoming was still a territory. The wings on each side of the original center section of the building were completed in 1890, and the legislative chamber wings were finished in 1917.

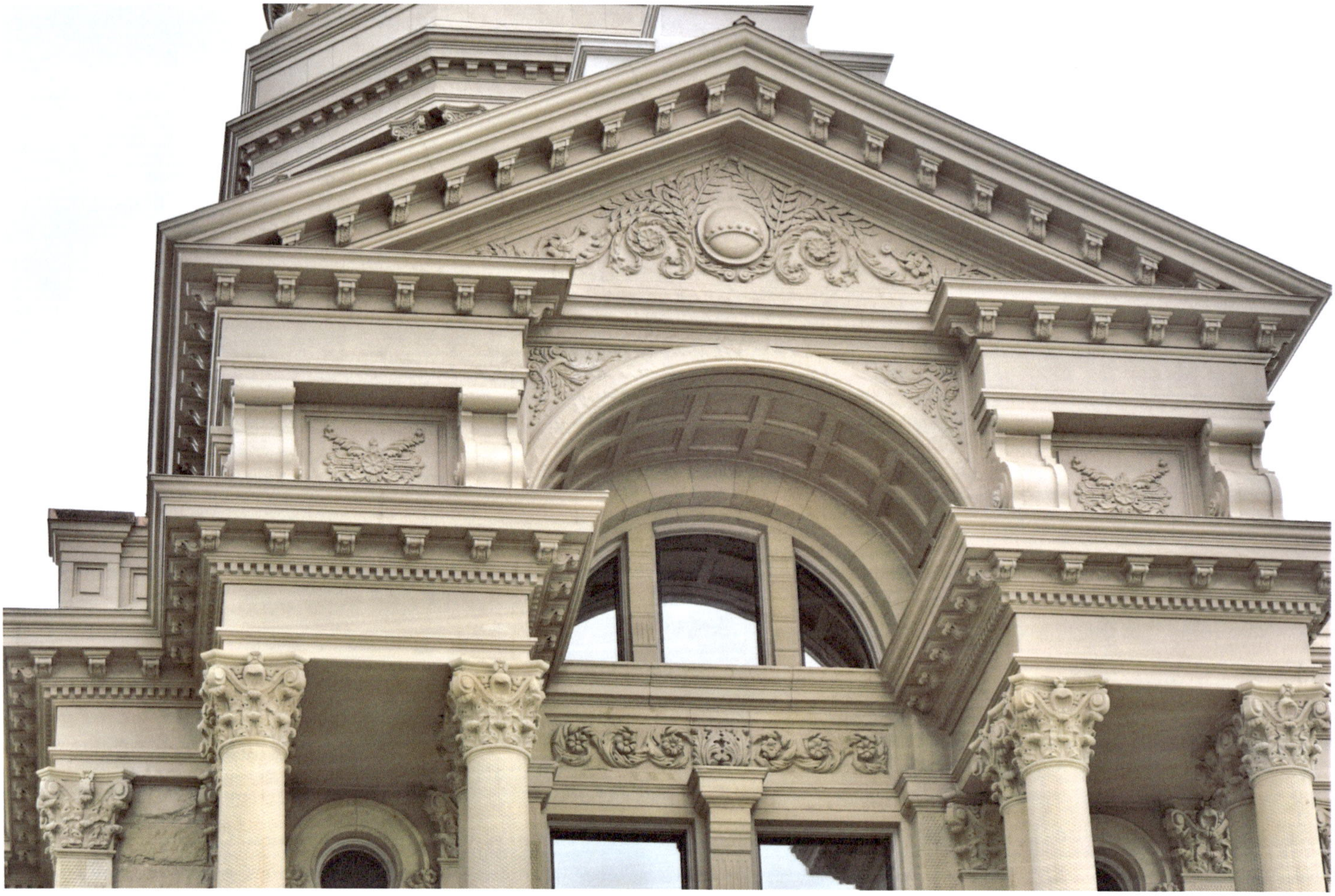

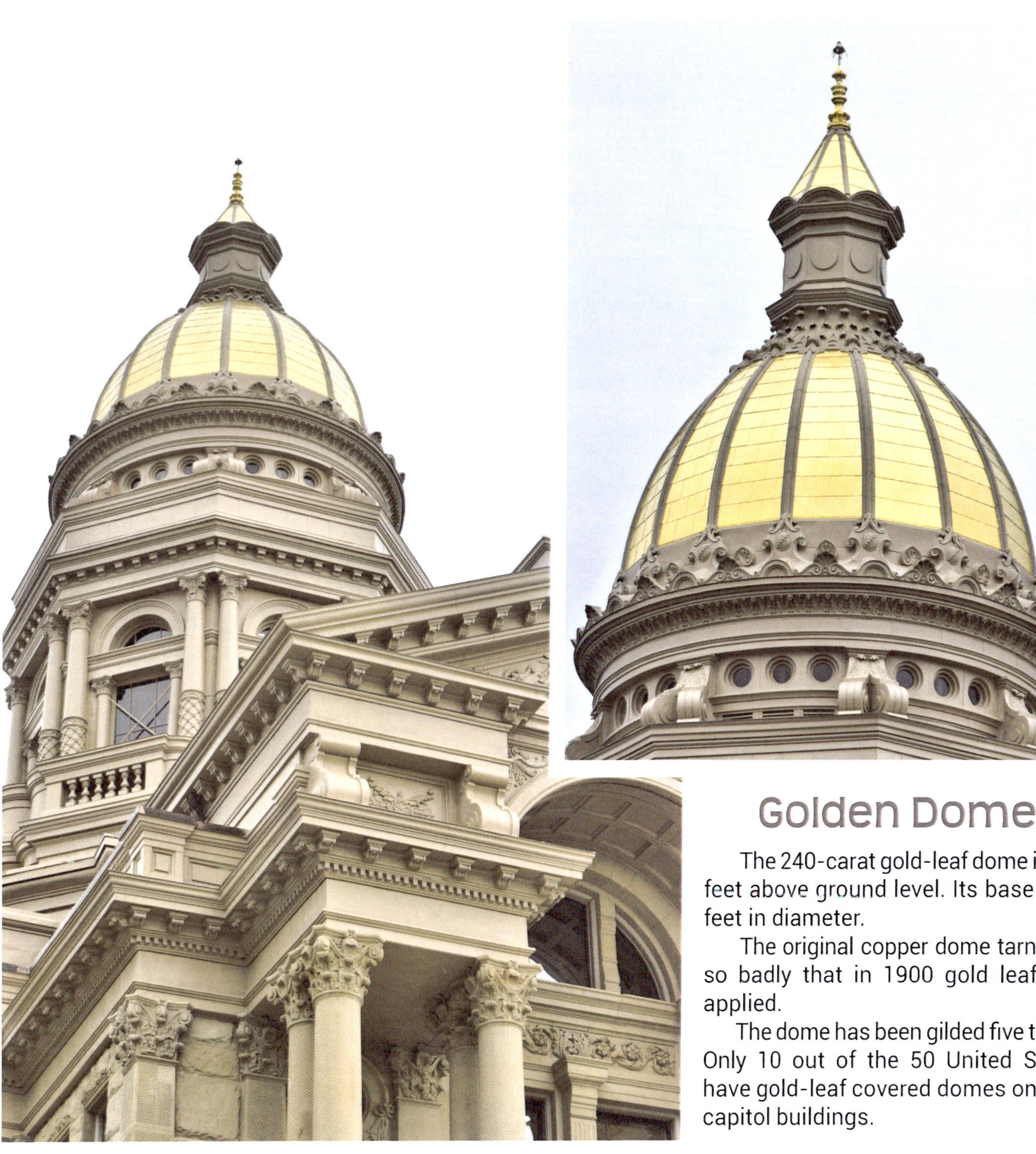

Golden Dome

The 240-carat gold-leaf dome is 146 feet above ground level. Its base is 50 feet in diameter.

The original copper dome tarnished so badly that in 1900 gold leaf was applied.

The dome has been gilded five times. Only 10 out of the 50 United States have gold-leaf covered domes on their capitol buildings.

Stained-glass, Tromp l'oeil Painting

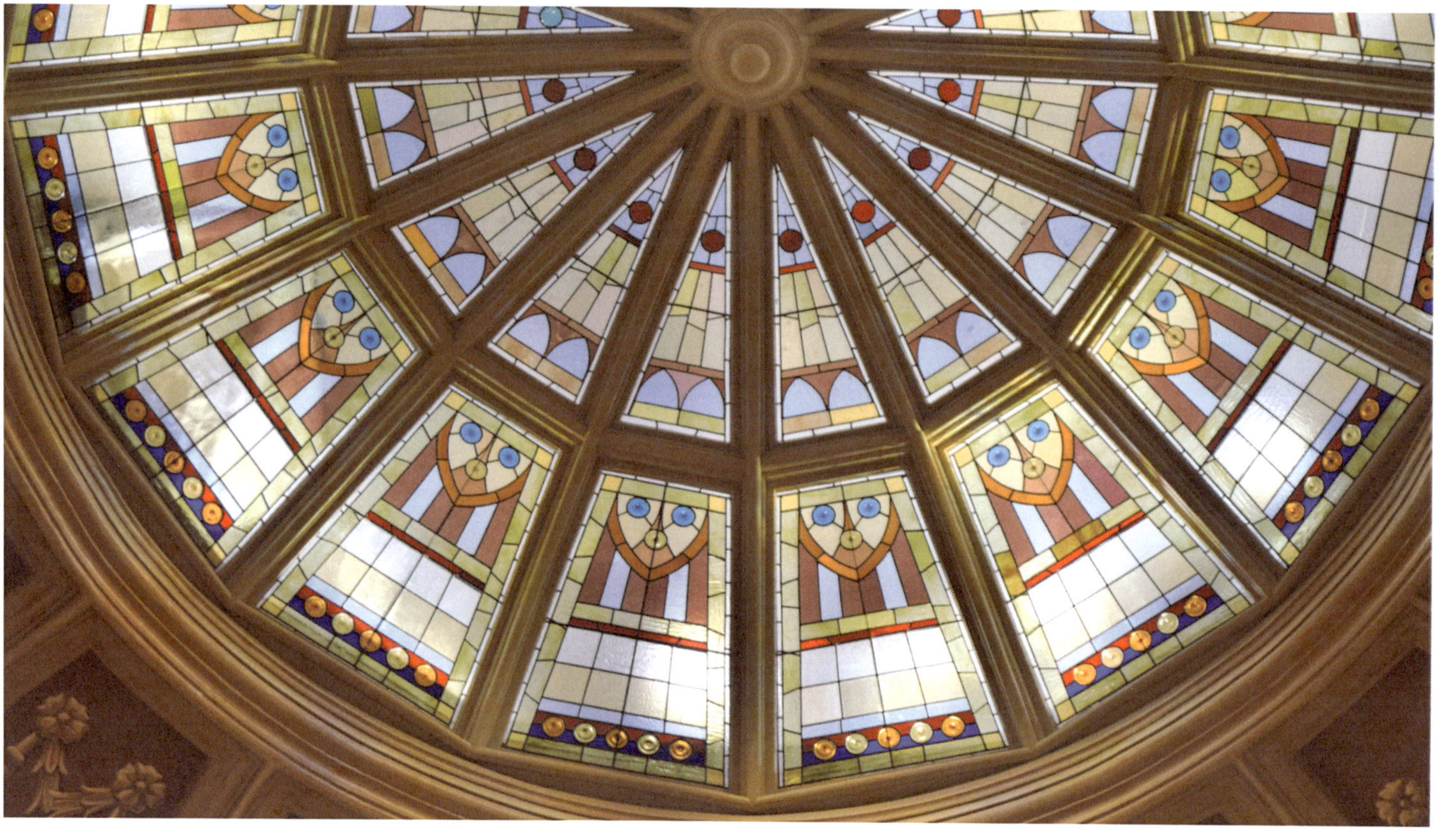

The English hand-made, double-cut stained-glass rotunda's dome interior is surrounded by trompe l'oeil painting.

This style of painting is an art technique that creates an optical illusion that the depicted objects exist in three dimensions.

During the capitol restoration, artists from Ever-Greene Architectural Arts hand-painted the 1888 patterns on canvas that were carefully installed.

Rotunda Dome

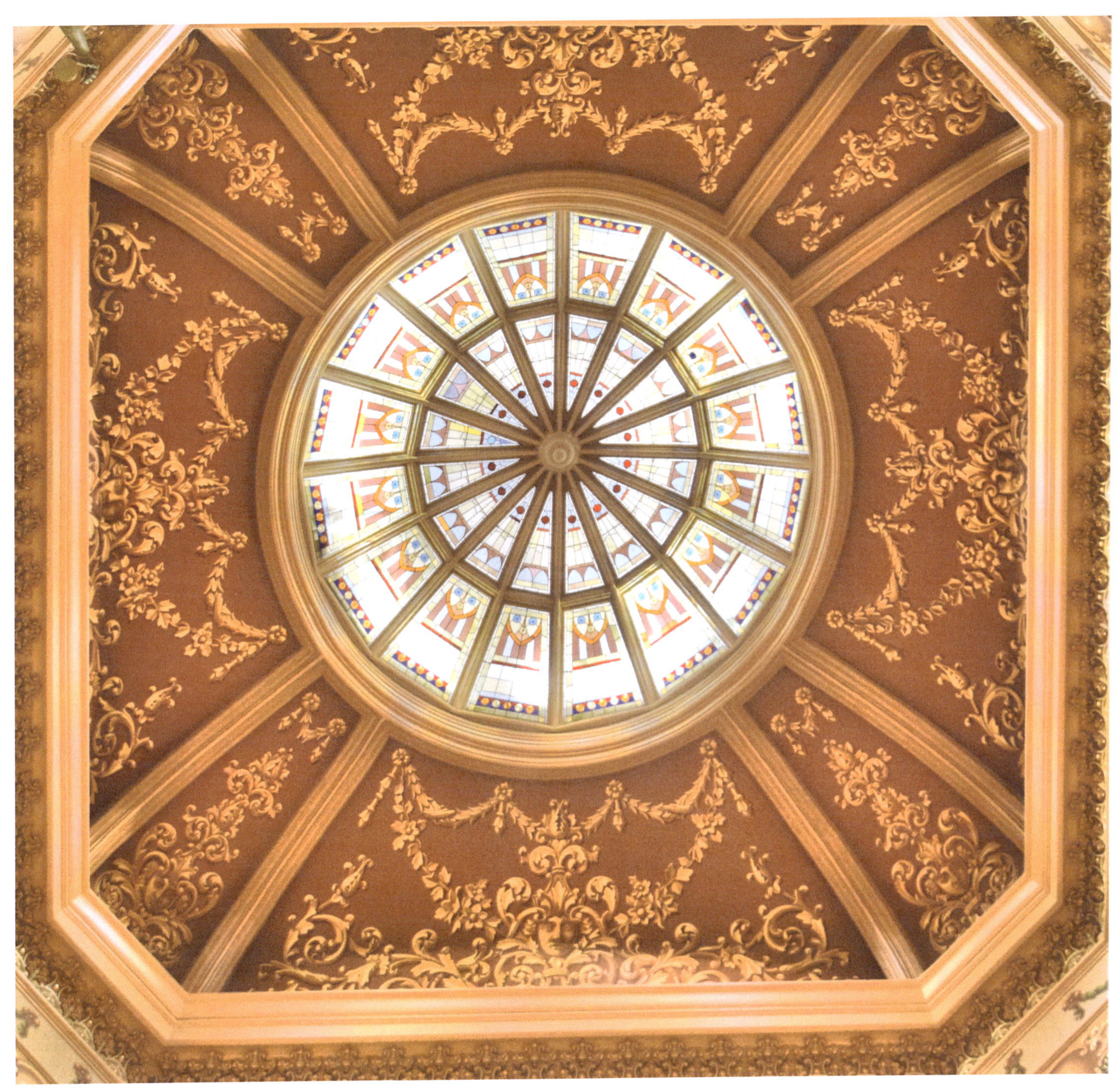

Cherrywood Grand Staircase

The cherrywood staircases were built by Amish craftsmen. It was no accident that the craftsmen, who assembled the baluster, endeavored to leave a lasting impression with one spindle placed upside down to symbolize humanity, reminding all that no person or law is perfect.

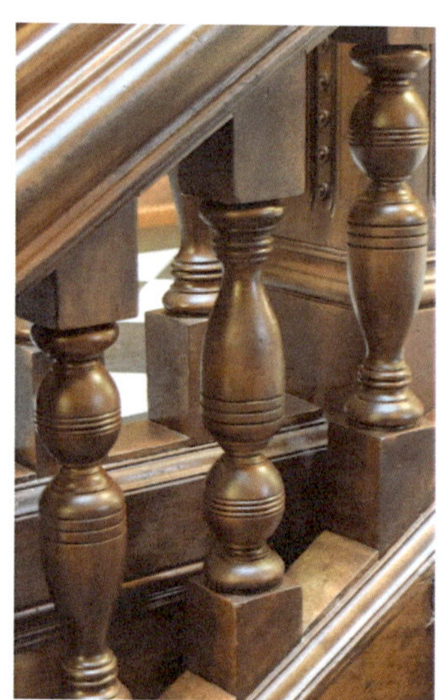

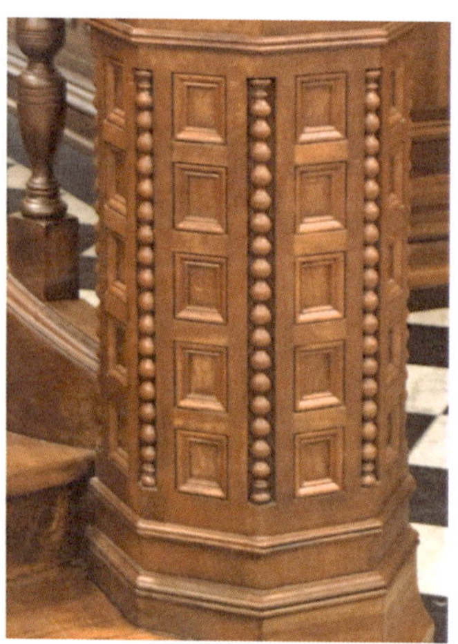

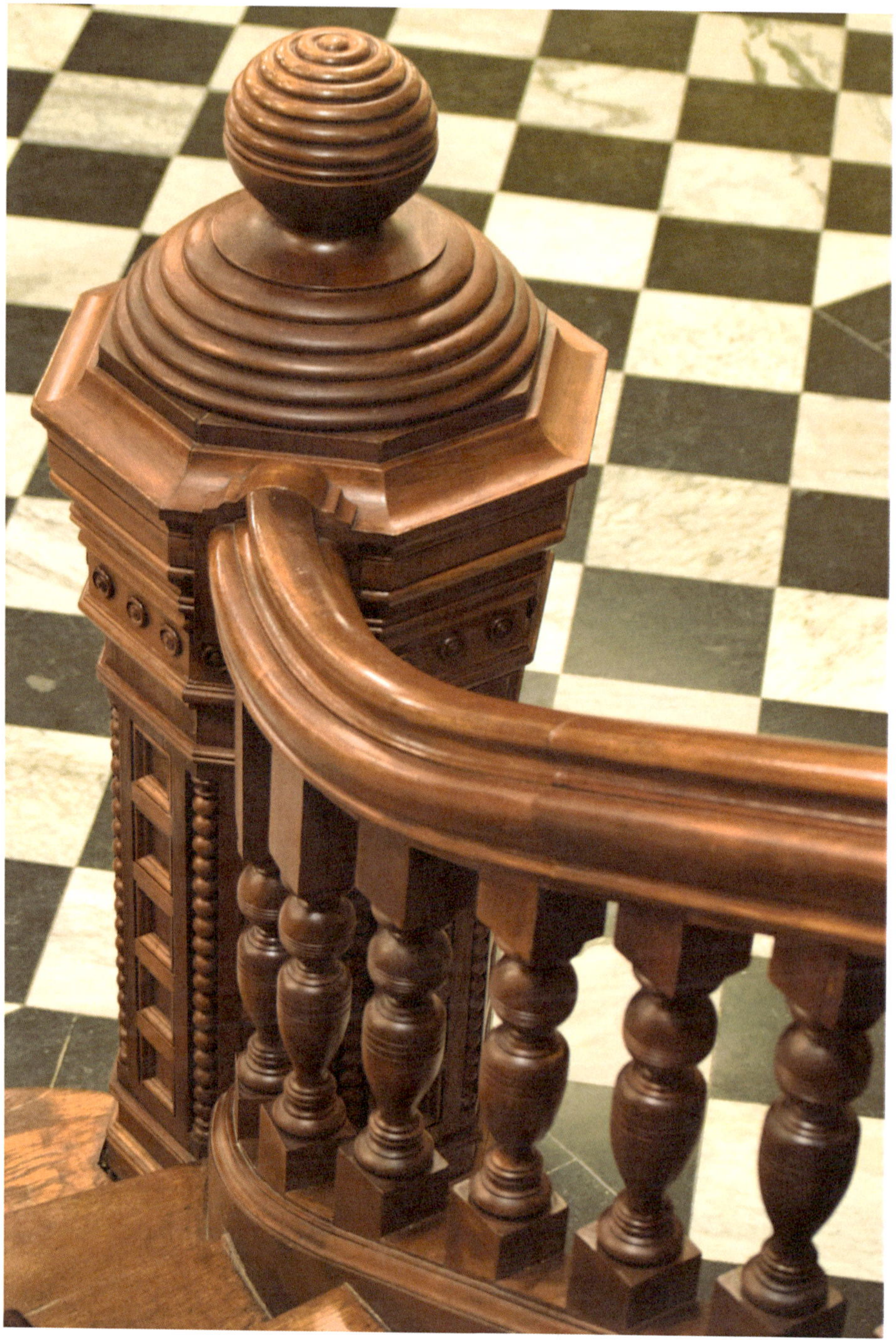

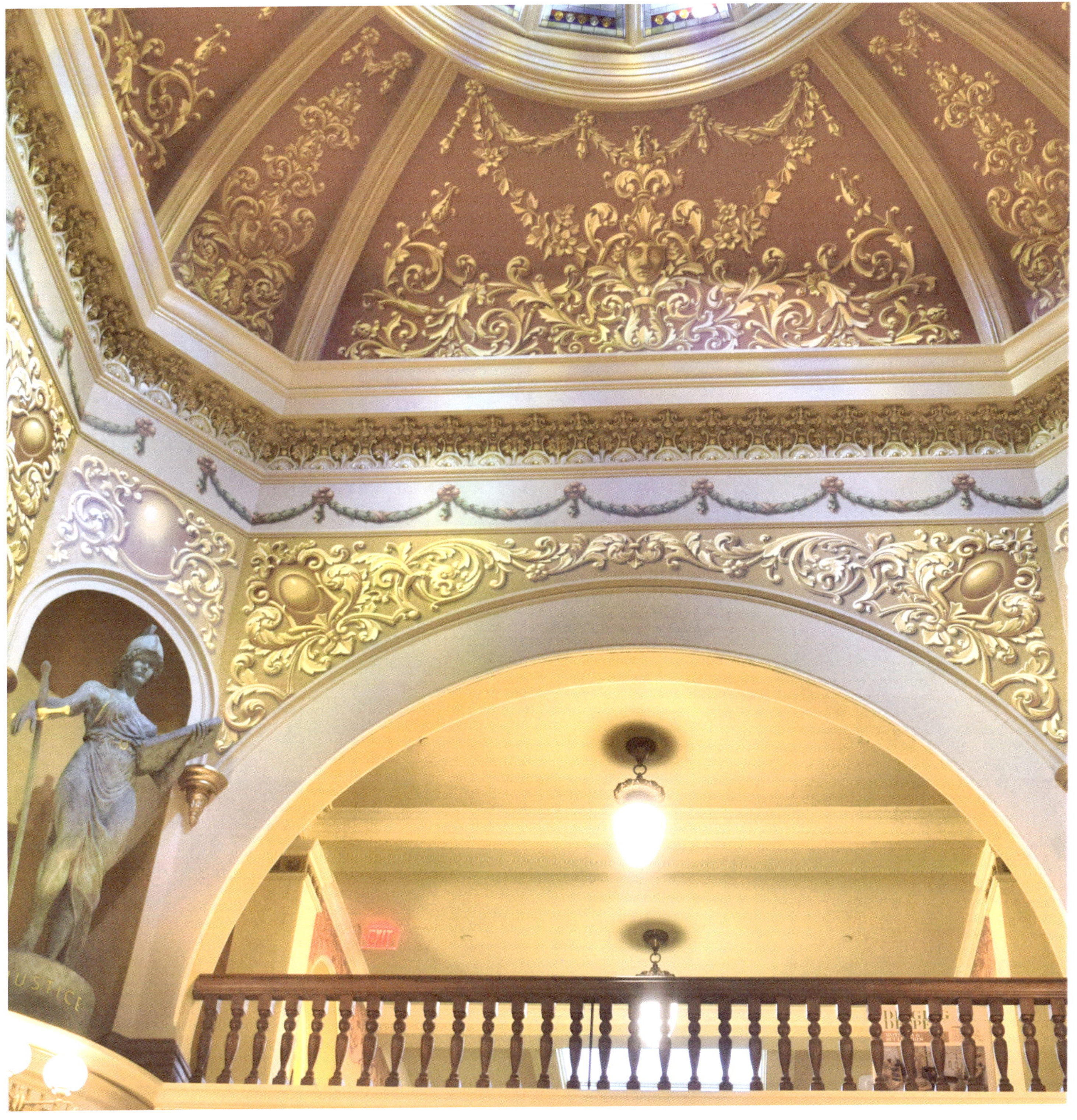

The Four Sister Statues

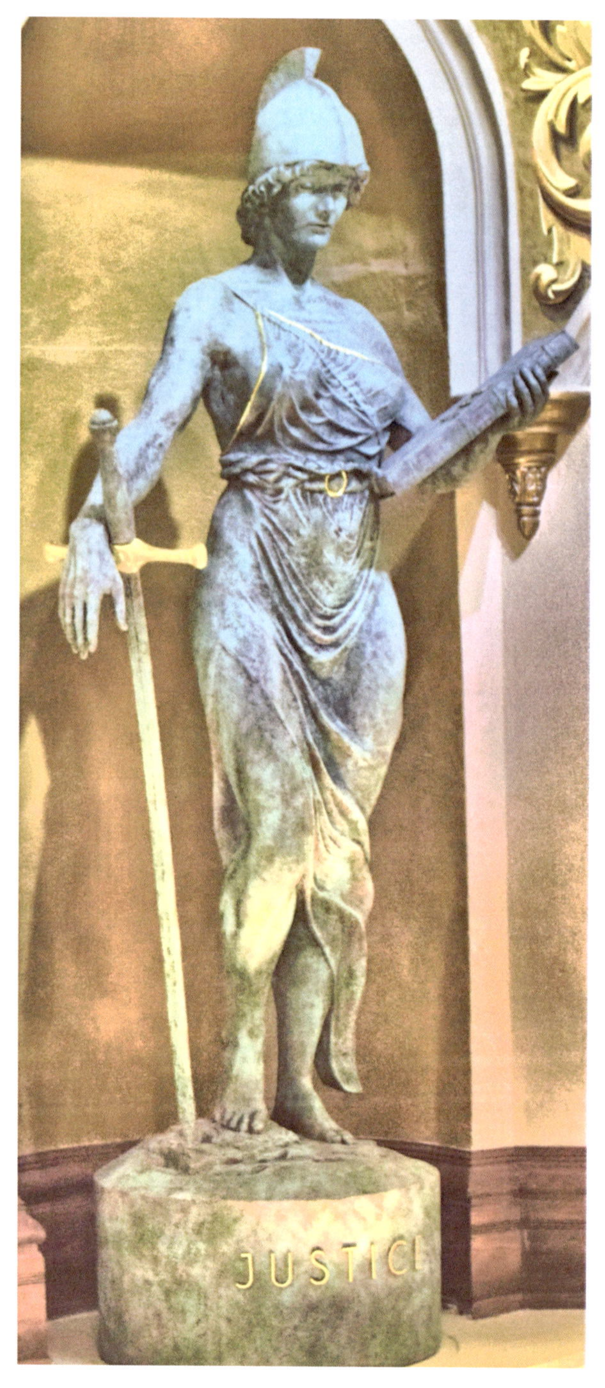

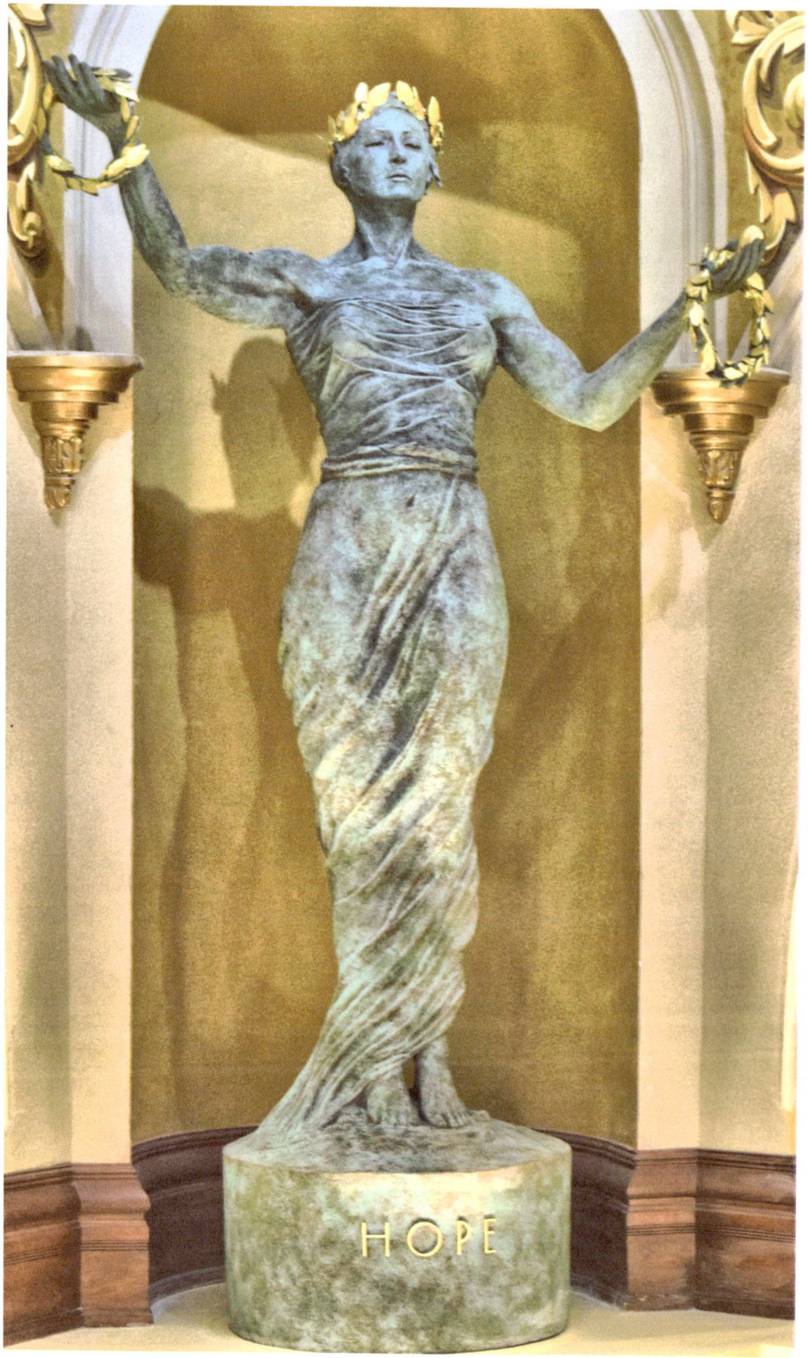

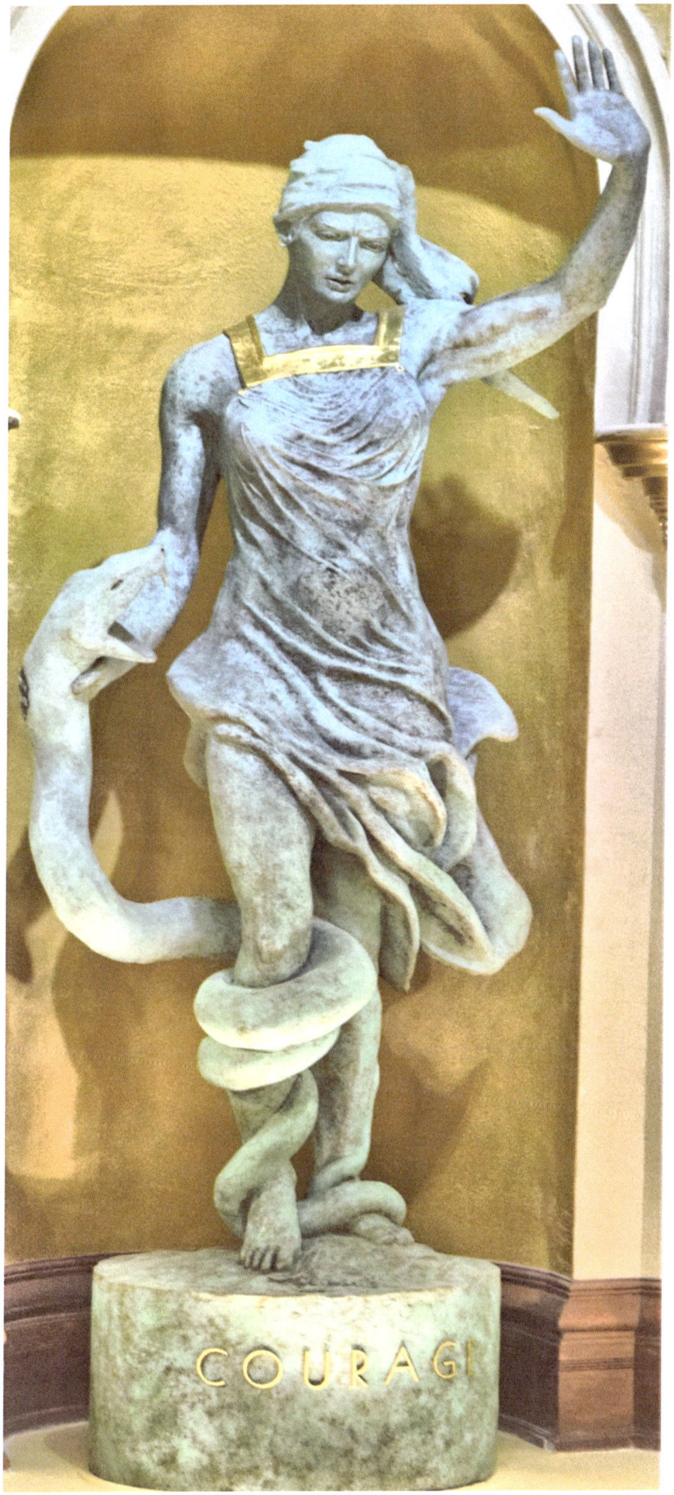

COURAGE

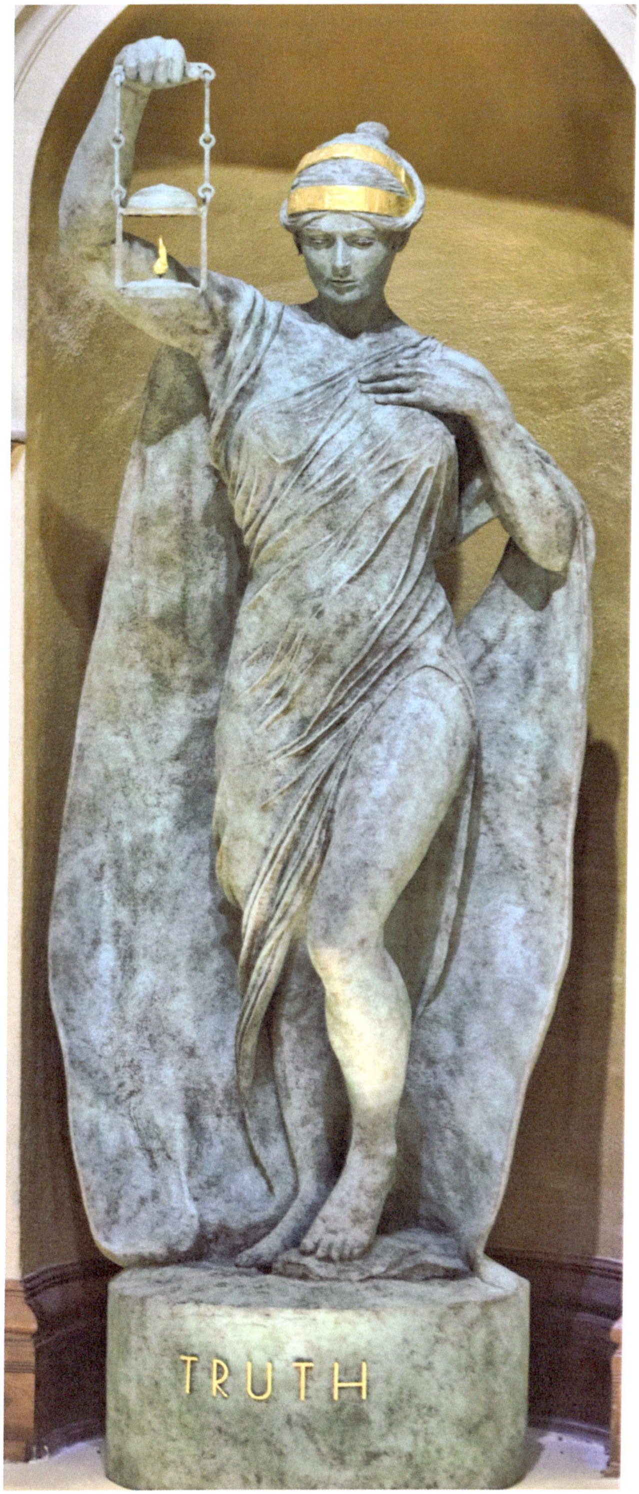

TRUTH

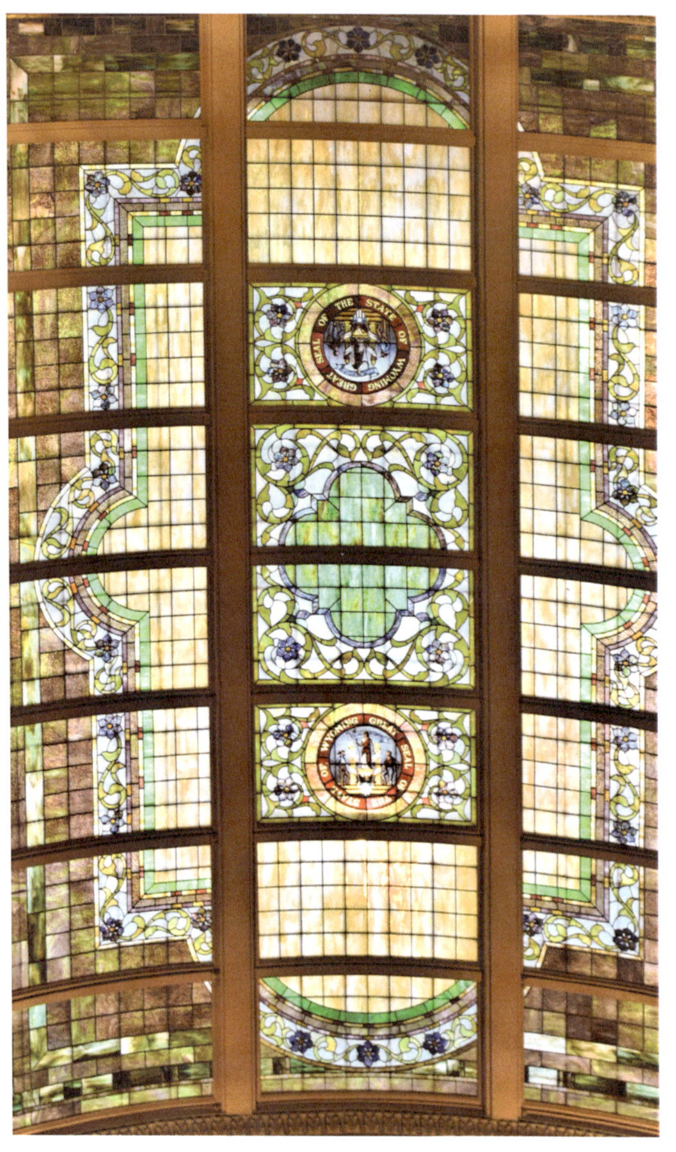

Senate Chamber

Both legislative chambers have Tiffany stained-glass ceilings featuring the state seal in the design.

The Senate chamber has two seals, while the House of Representative chamber has one in the middle of its design.

Each chamber has murals by artist Allen Tupper True depicting the people that settled the Wyoming Territory.

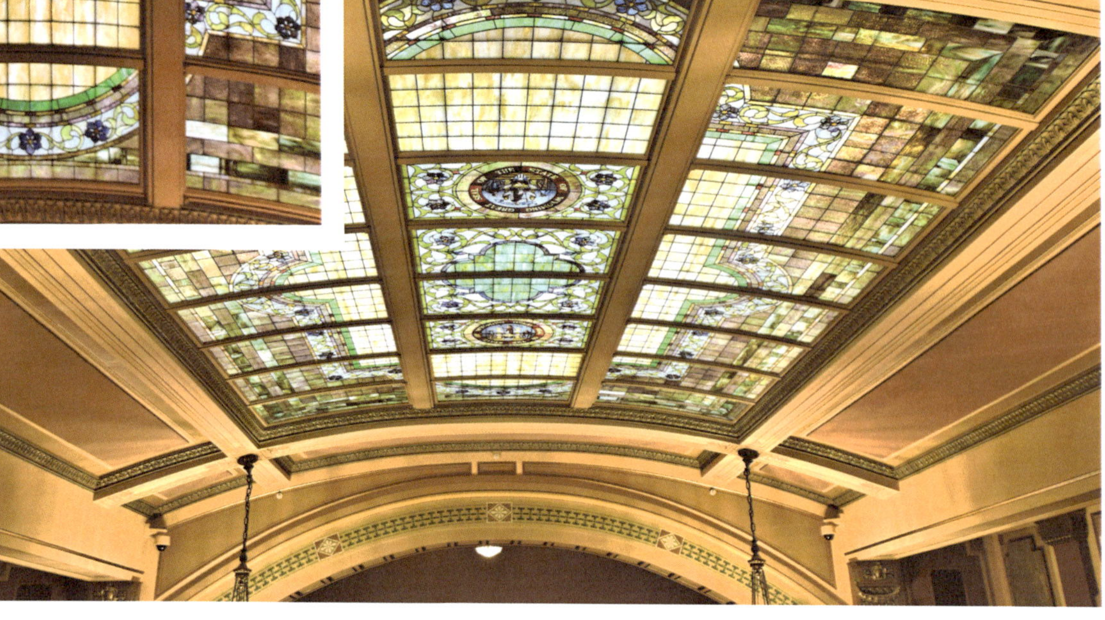

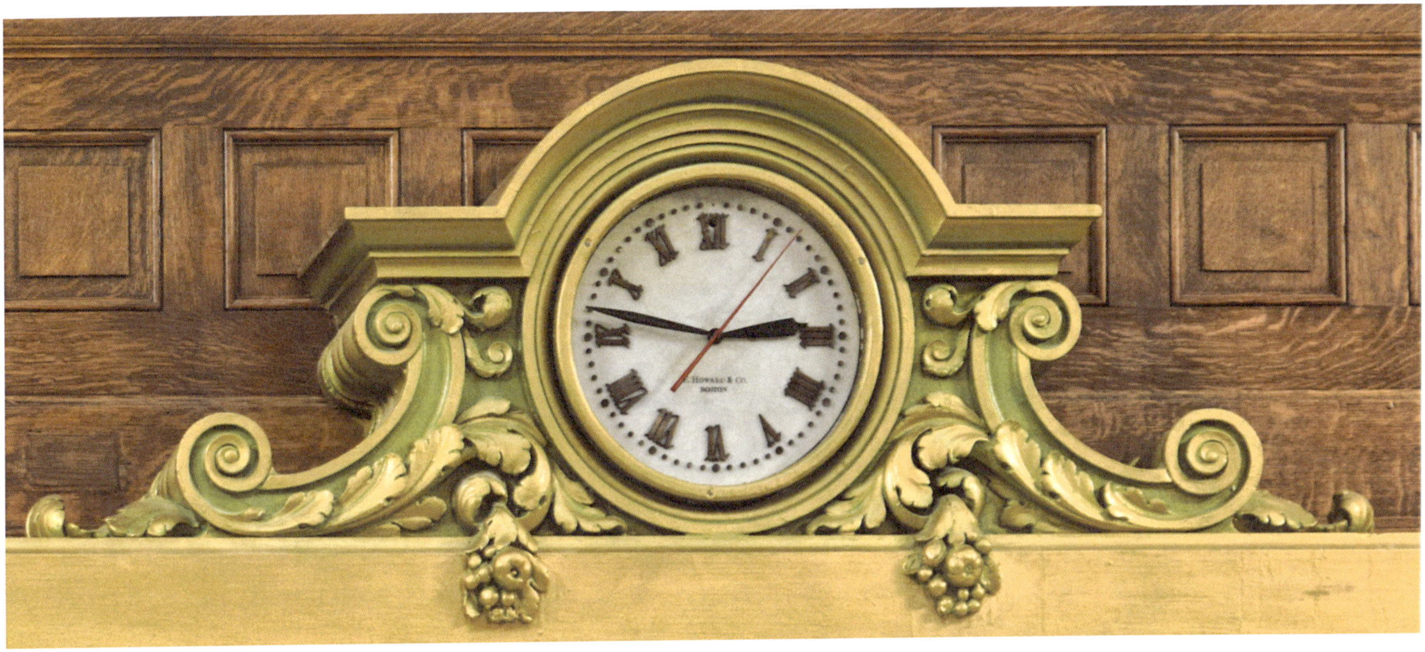

Howard & Co.
BOSTON

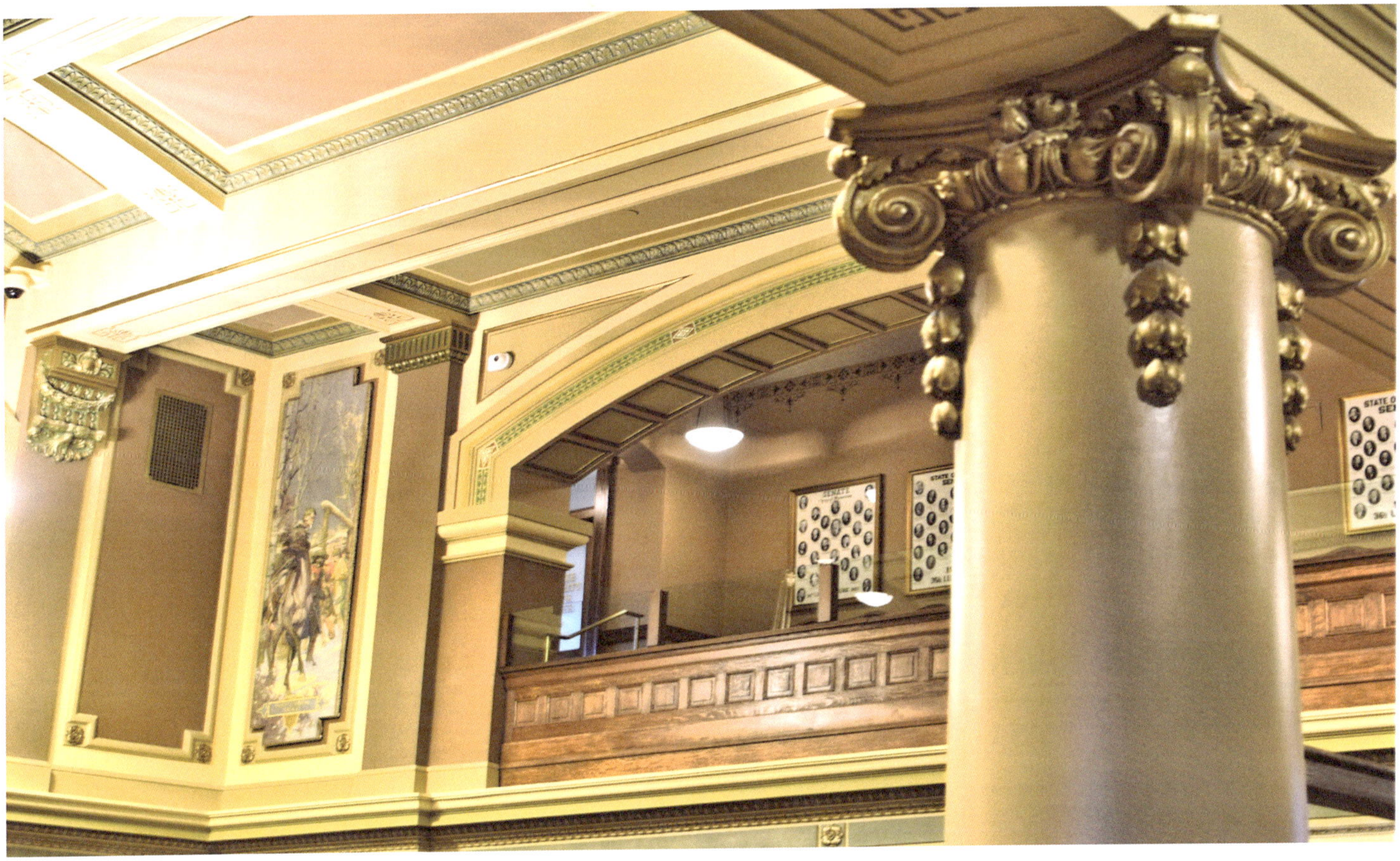

House of Representatives Chamber

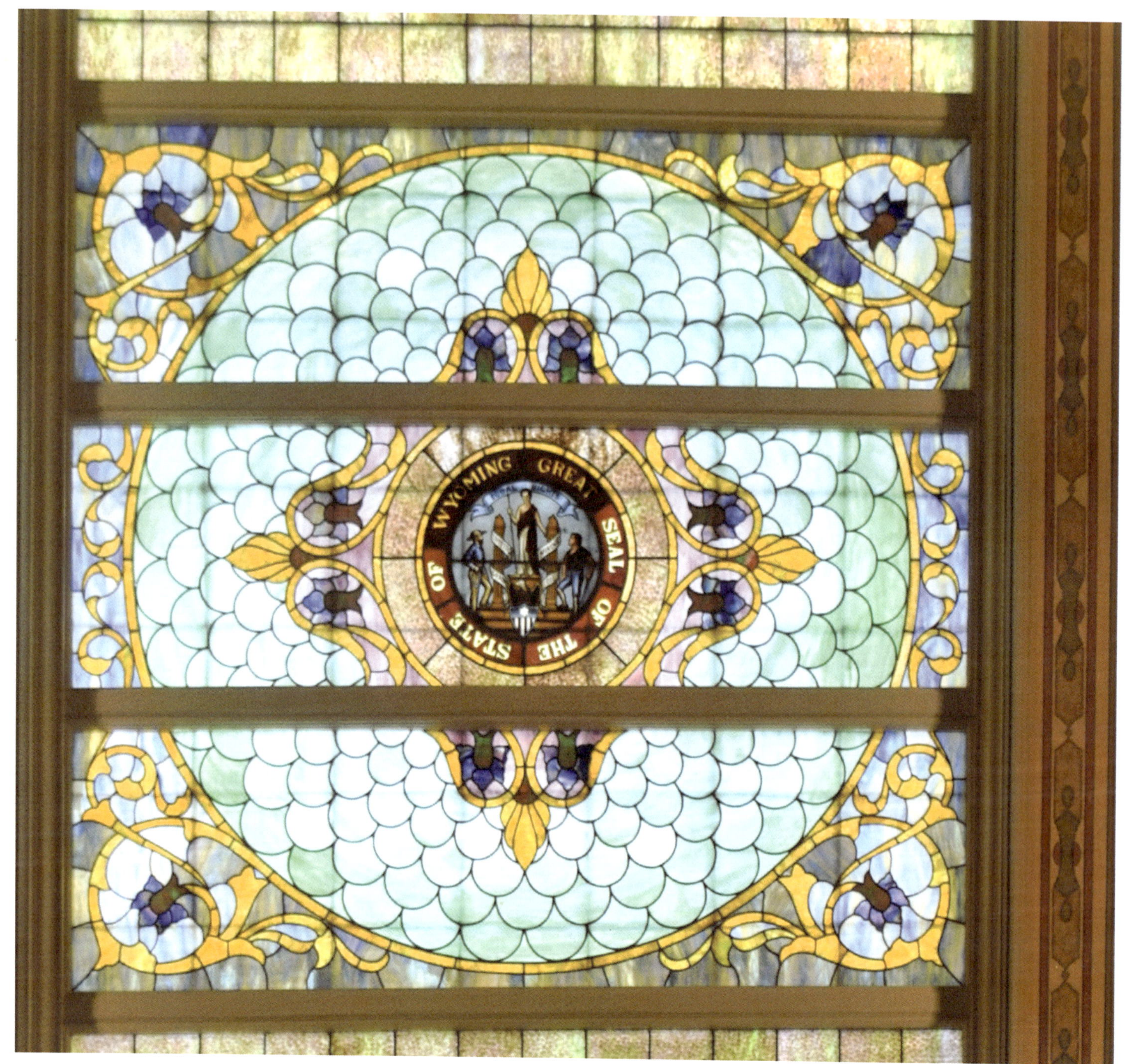

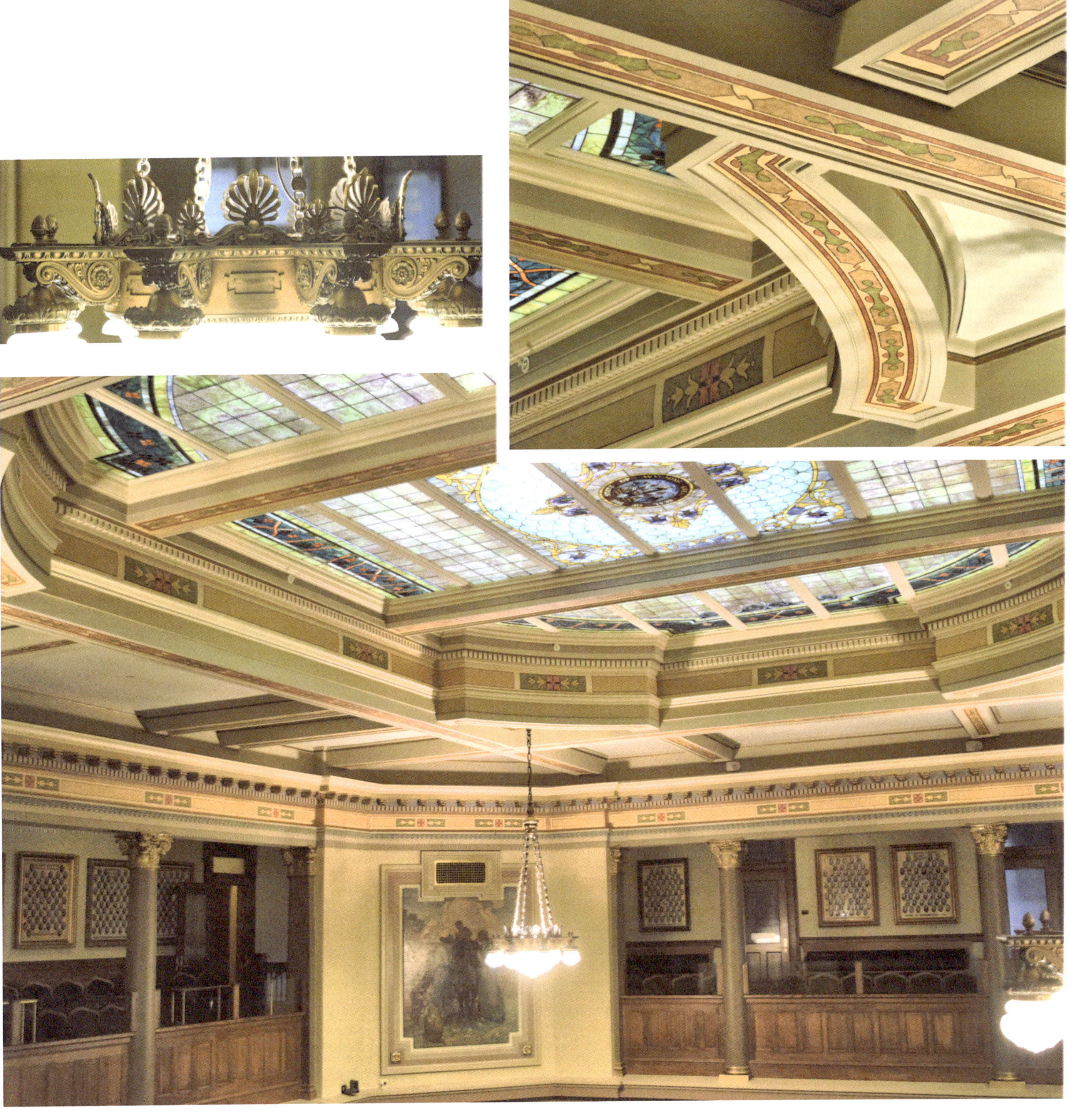

Legislative Chamber Murals

Eight large murals by Allen Tupper True in the Senate and House of Representatives chambers were the artist's first big assignment, which were finished in 1918. The murals depict various aspects of the culture, history and industry of Wyoming.

The House murals are titled "Trappers," "Cattlemen," "Homesteaders," and "Stagecoach." The murals in the Senate chamber are titled "Indian Chief Cheyenne," "Frontier Cavalry Officer," "Pony Express Rider," and "Railroad Builders Surveyors."

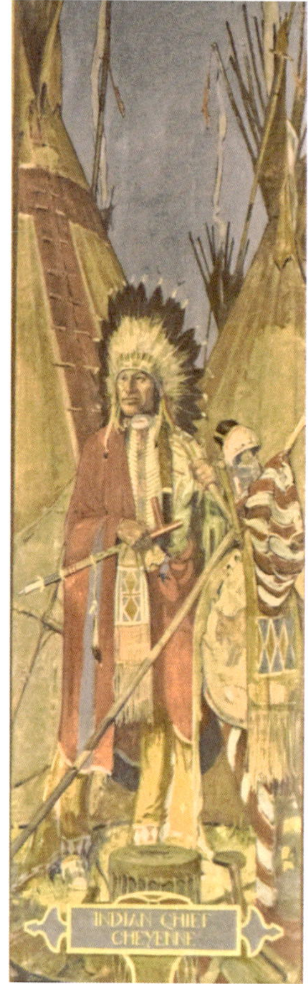

Indian Chief Cheyenne

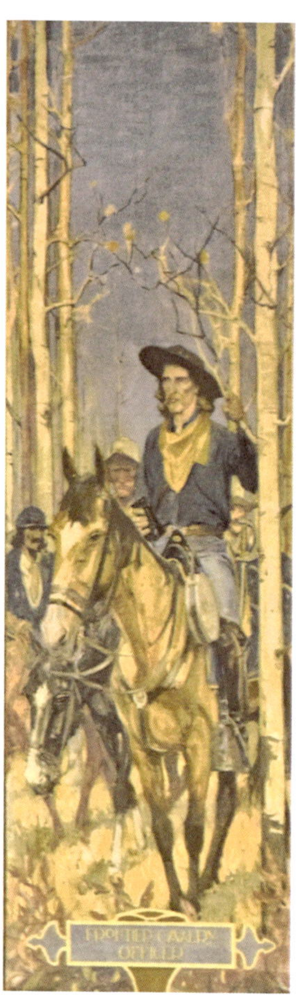

Frontier Cavalry Officer

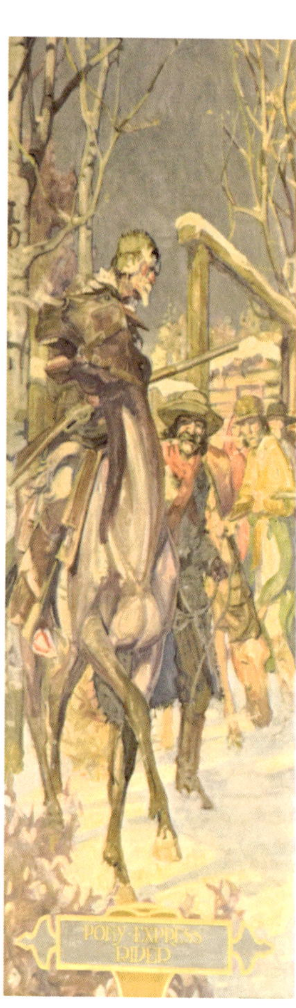

Pony Express Rider

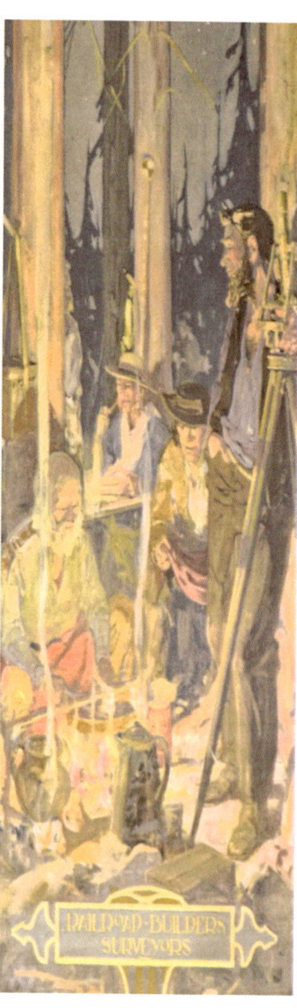

Railroad Builders Surveyors

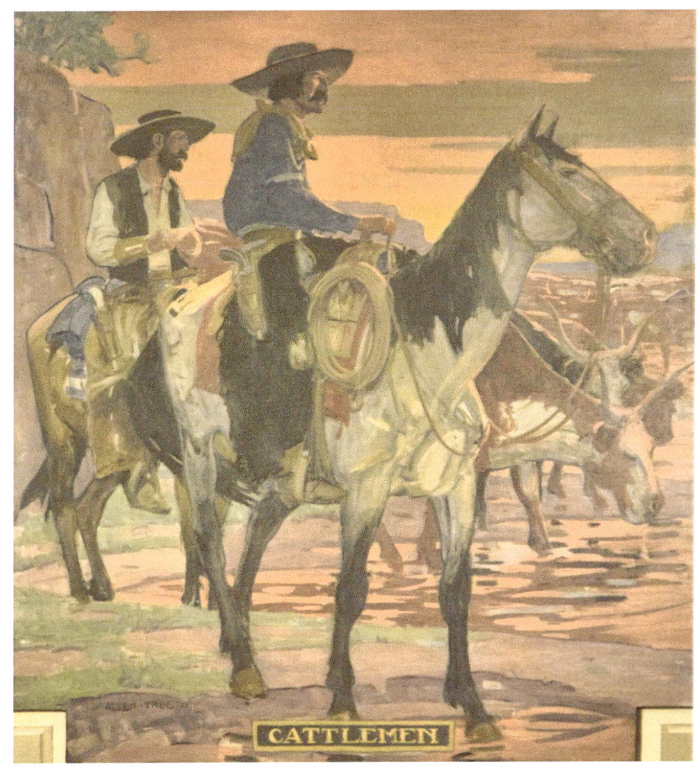
CATTLEMEN

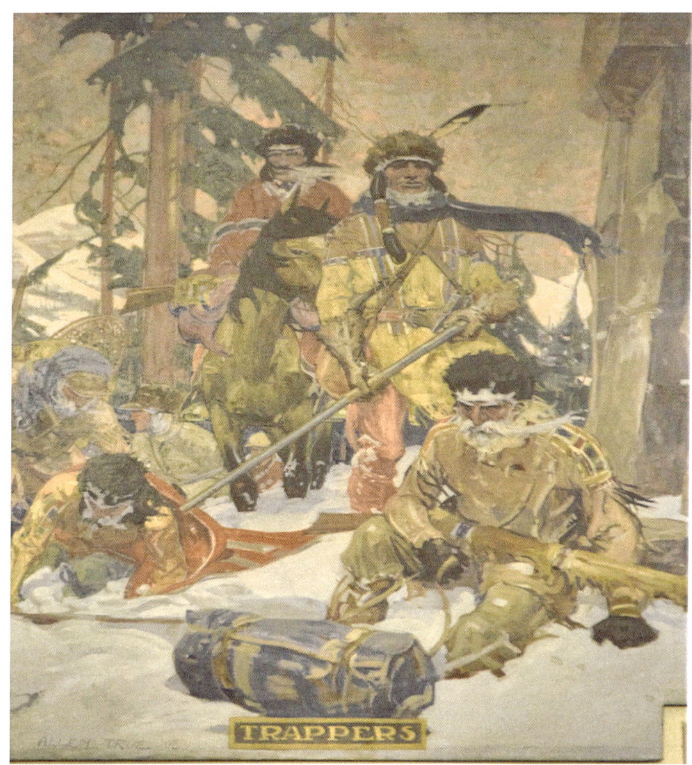
TRAPPERS

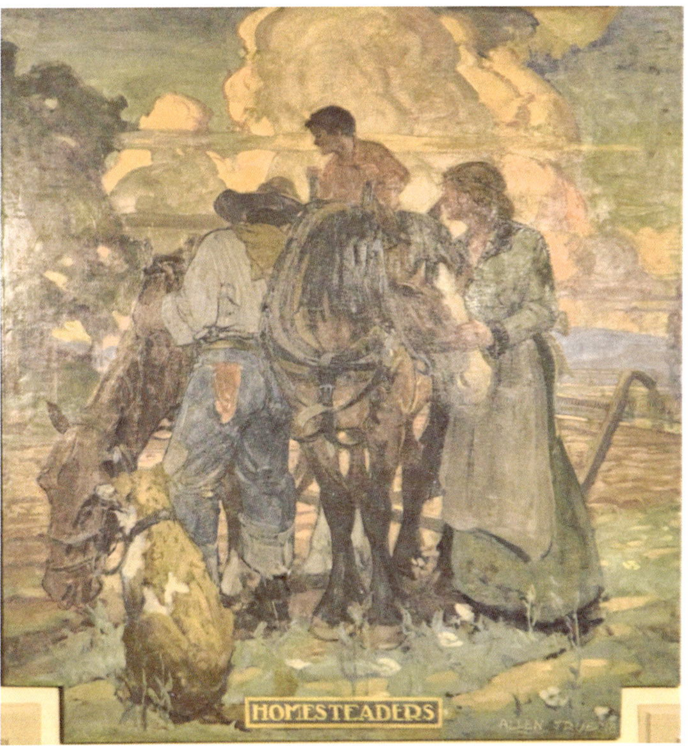
HOMESTEADERS

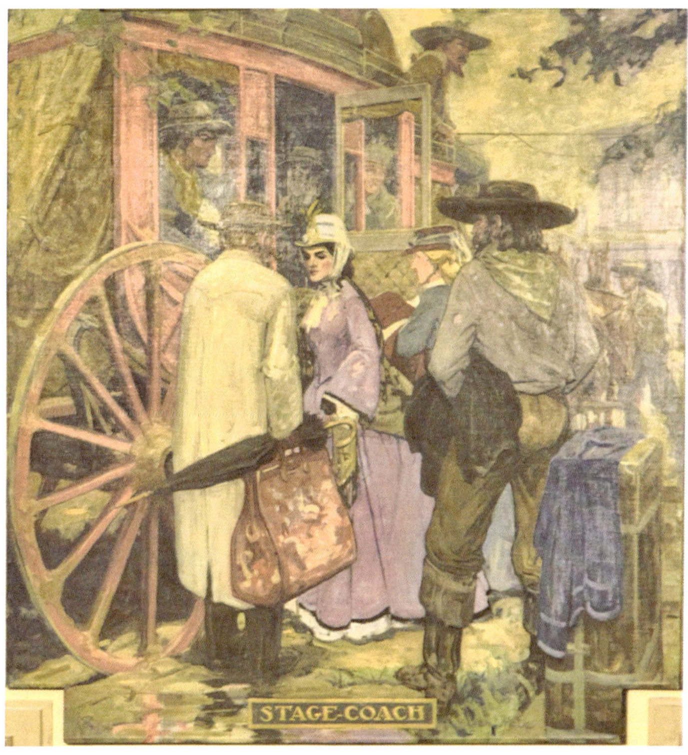
STAGE-COACH

Historic Supreme Court Chamber

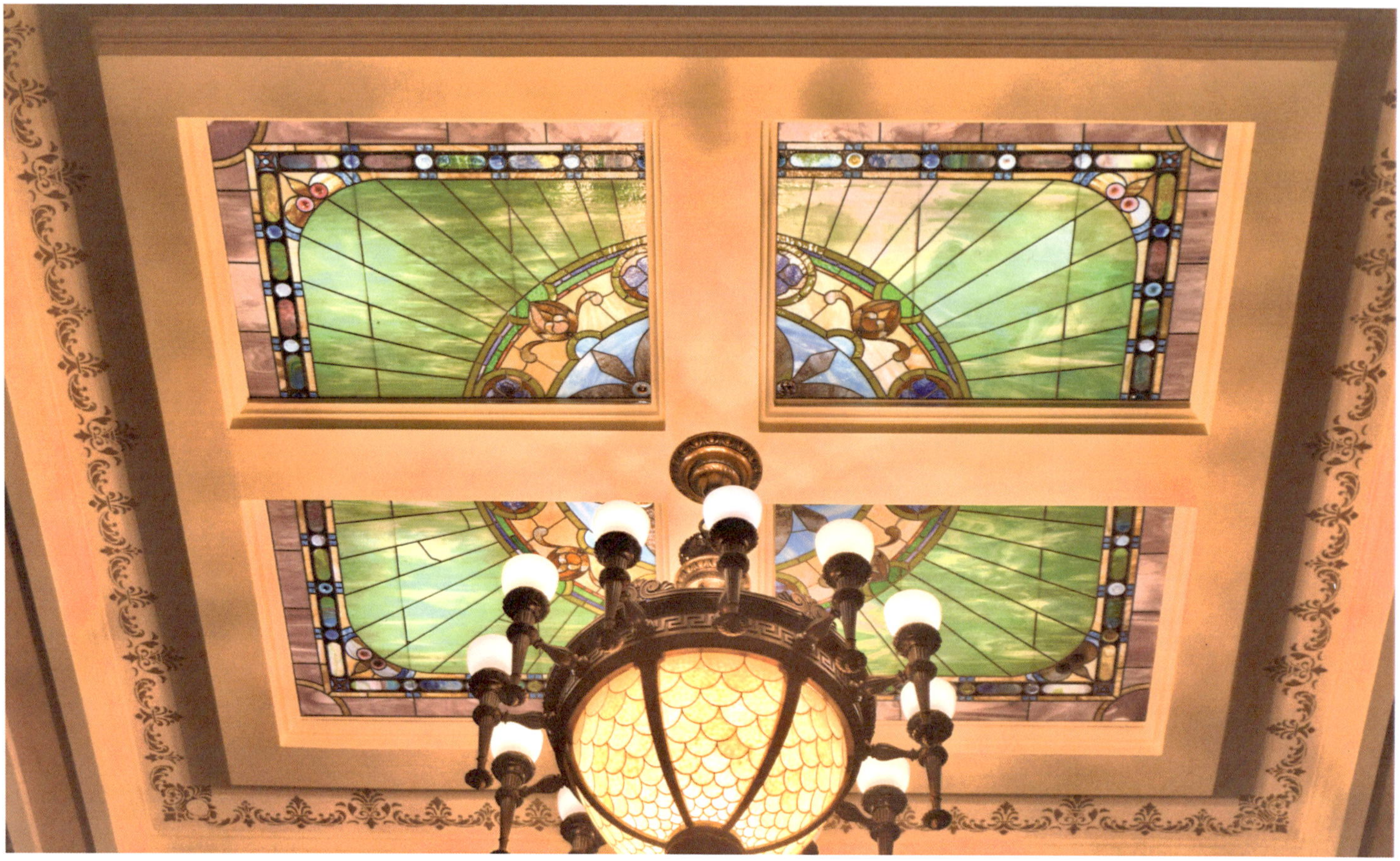

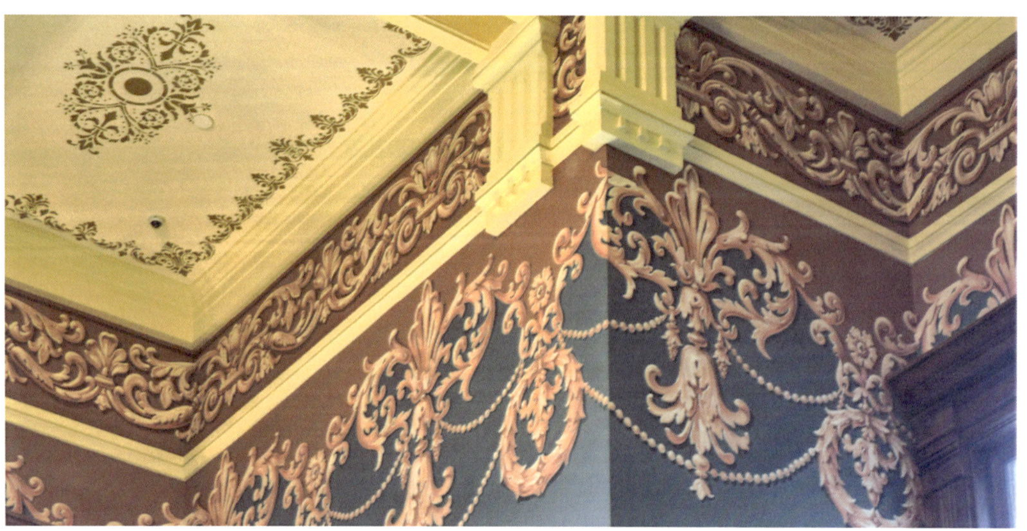

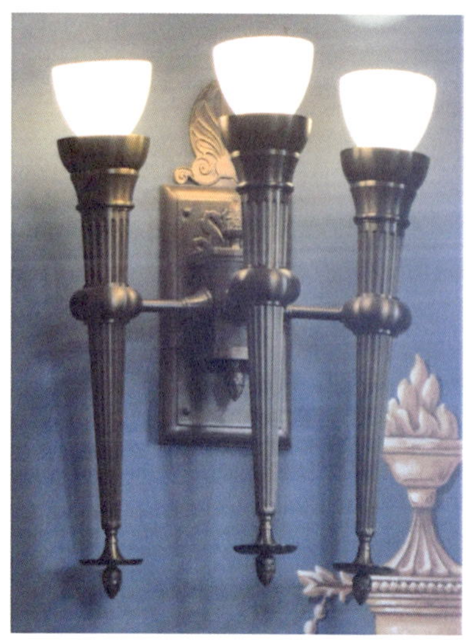

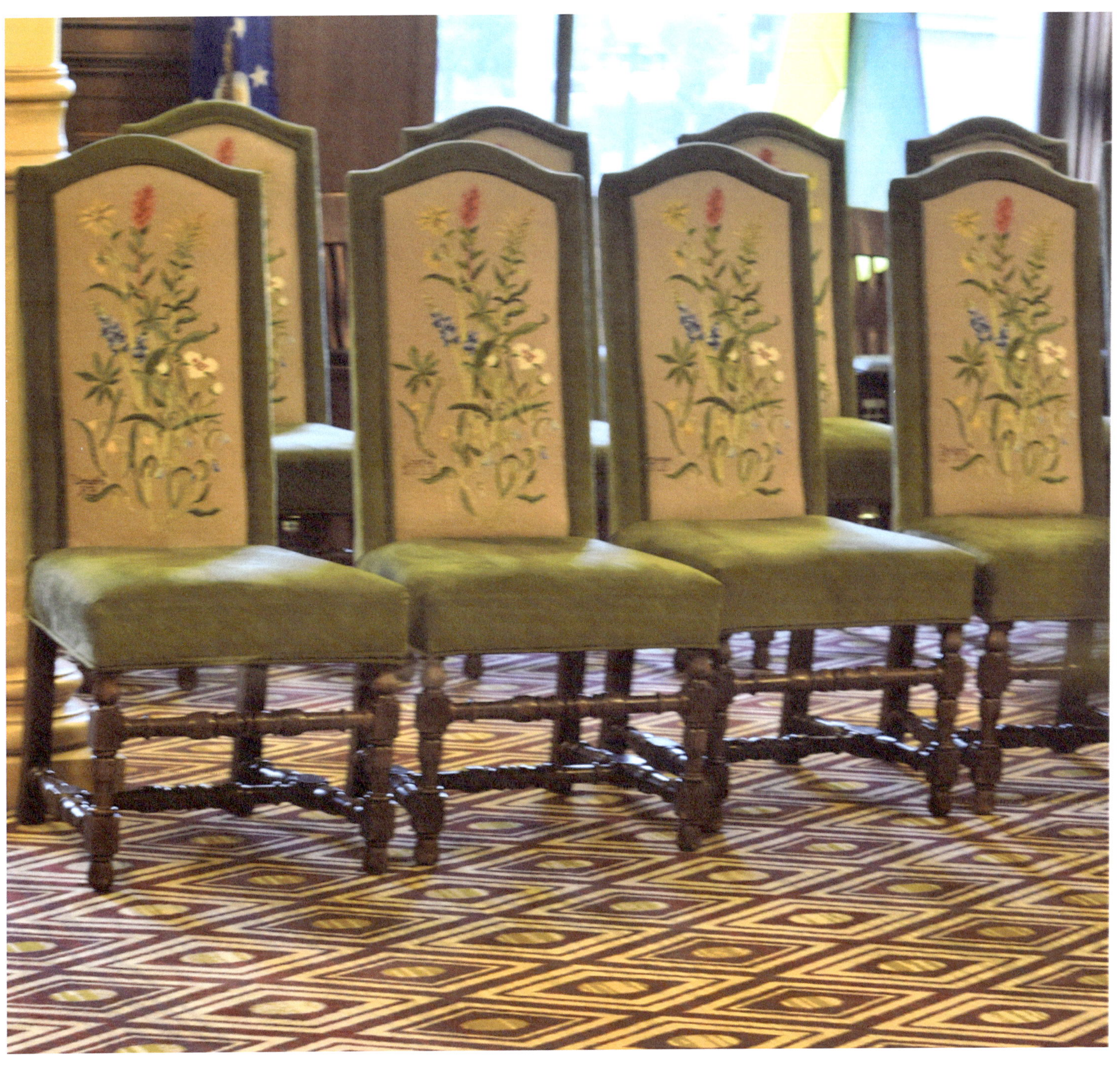

Historic Vault Art

Vibrant oil paintings on six vault doors were uncovered during the capitol restoration. Various designs of gold pinstripe-stenciling surround each of the paintings.

EverGreene Architectural Arts discovered the paintings by carefully removing several layers of paint. Uncovering each door took between one and two days.

The six Mosler Safe and Lock Co vaults date back to before 1891 and were placed during the 1888 or 1890 building phases. Mosler Safe Company of Cincinnati, Ohio, was one of the largest manufacturers of safes and vault doors.

The artists of the six beautiful paintings remain unknown. Elaborate decorations on vault doors were not unusual for the time.

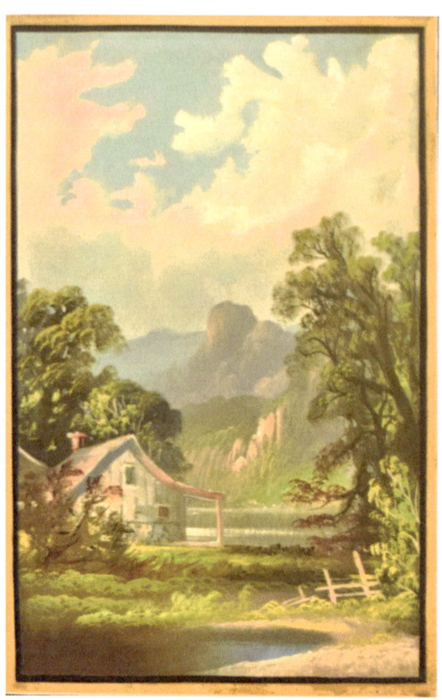

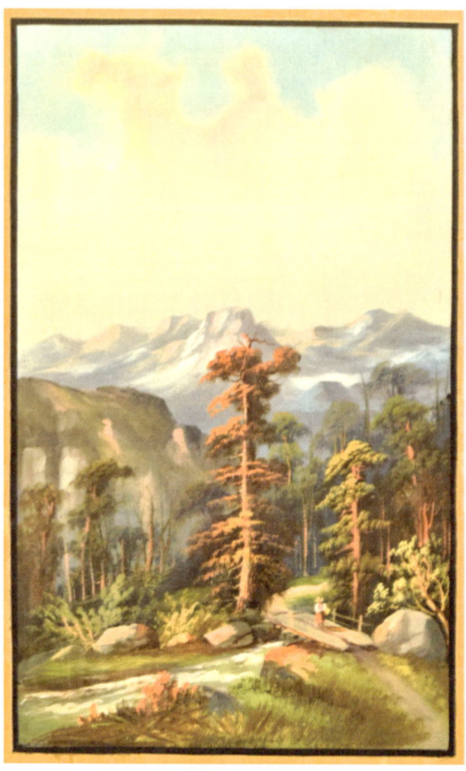

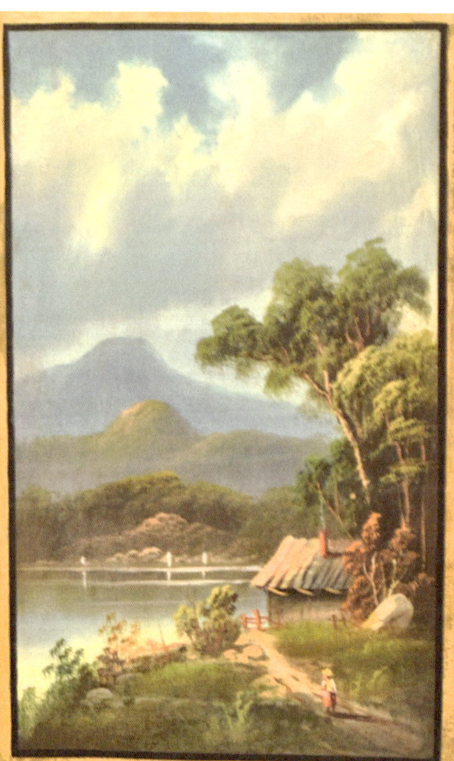

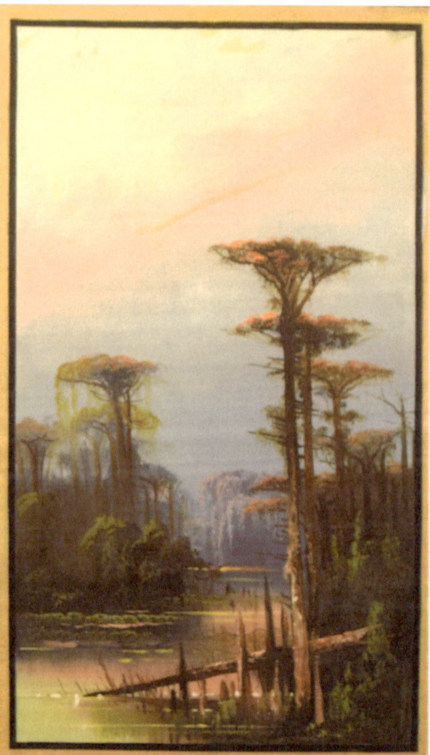

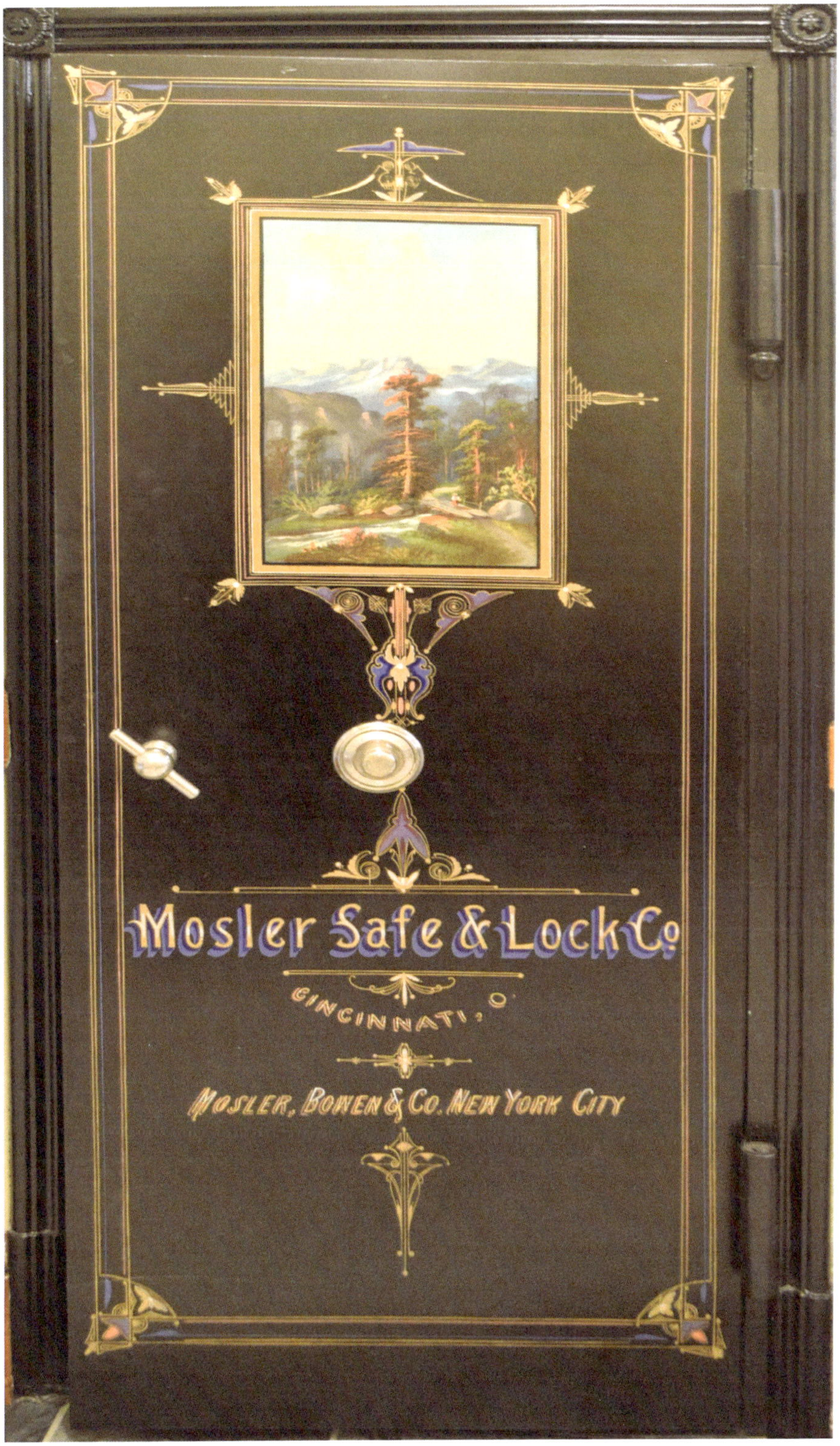

Mosler Safe & Lock Co
CINCINNATI, O.
MOSLER, BOWEN & CO. NEW YORK CITY

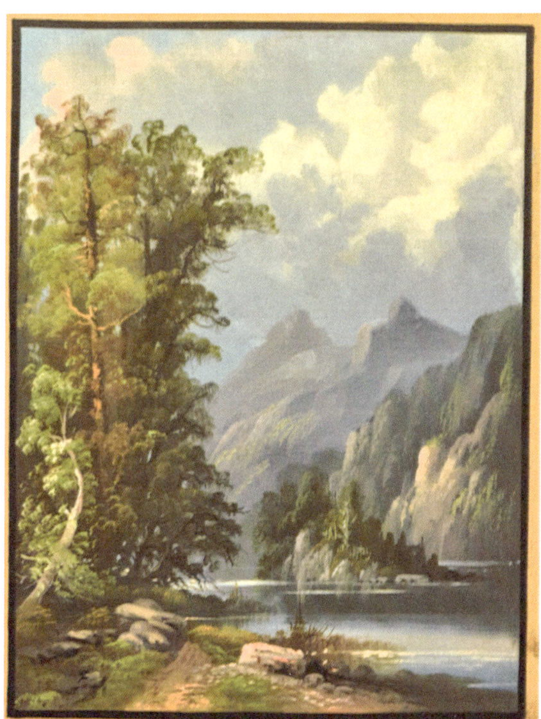

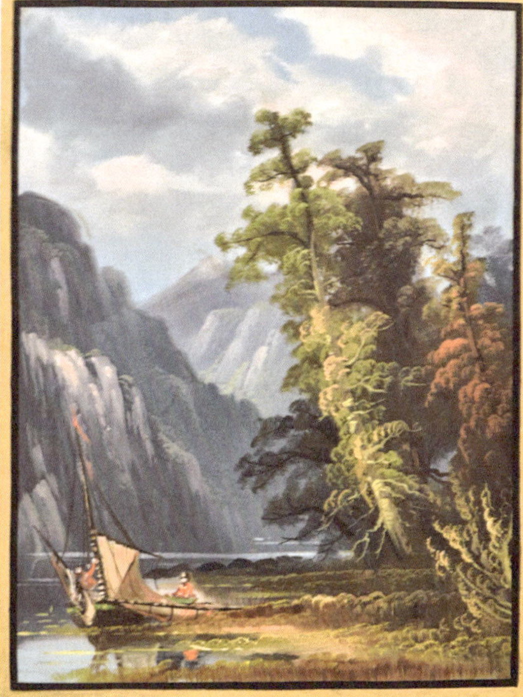

Wyoming State Seal

The Great Seal of the State of Wyoming was adopted by the second legislature in 1893, revised by the sixteenth legislature in 1921.

The two dates on the Great Seal, 1869 and 1890 commemorate the organization of the Territorial government and Wyoming's admission to the Union.

The draped figure in the center holds a staff from which flows a banner bearing the words, "Equal Rights," and symbolizes the political status women have always enjoyed in Wyoming.

The male figures typify the livestock and mining industries of the state.

On top of the pillars rest lamps from which burn the Light of Knowledge. Scrolls encircling the two pillars bear the words, Oil, Mines, Livestock, and Grain, four of Wyoming's major industries.

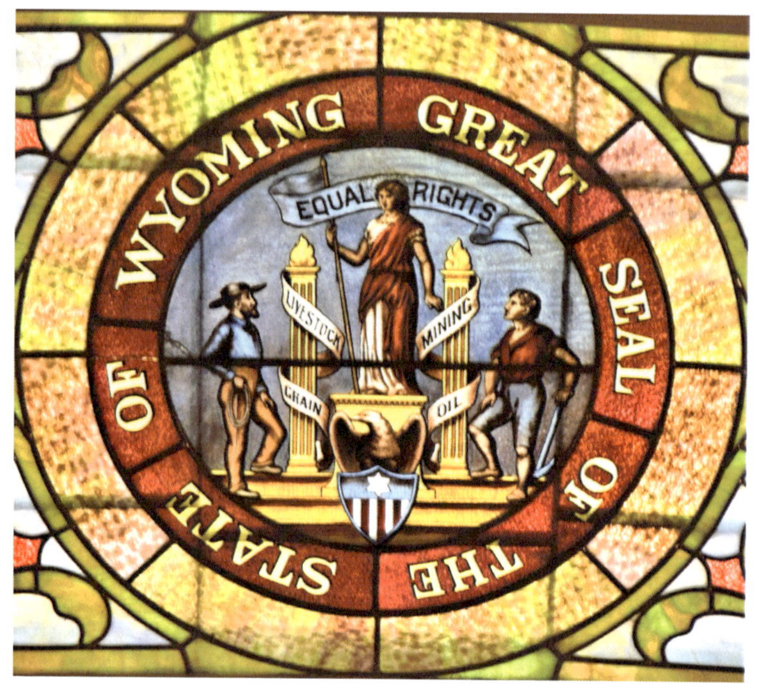

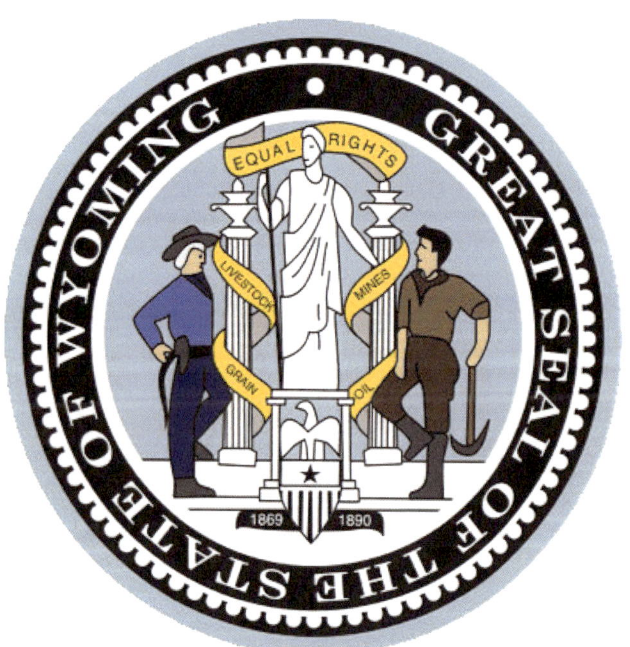

About the Photographer

Jane Moorman describes herself as an adventurer who loves to drive the backroads to see what there is to see.

During her 30-year journalism career, Jane honed her photographic skills as a photojournalist, including covering high school sporting events.

A friend once said, "I wish I could see the world as Jane sees it. Finding the beauty in things that most of us don't take time to see."

Upon retiring in 2021, Jane decided there is a lot of her native country she had not visited, including each state's capitol, so she began her journey of exploring the USA.

Jane currently lives in Albuquerque, New Mexico, but says her real home is on the road.